Top Notch Couples:

An Affair Workbook for the Person Who Cheated

Rationale

The concept in writing this book is that so many people have had an affair and report feeling disoriented. They feel tremendous guilt, the kind that paralyzes them rather than moves them toward making things better. They are so disoriented, they do not know where to turn and how to get out of, or through, the situation. This is simply the first step. Go to counseling. Talk to someone who is healthy and knows how to give you guidance through this. This workbook is simply the beginning of the process.

I thank the numerous people in my practice who have given me permission to share their story as a composite. That means none of the stories is just one couple, it is a combination of numerous couples and names have been changed to keep a level of privacy.

Goal

If I do this well, then the people who have had the affair will be able to say the equivalent, "This is why I had the affair. I am so terribly sorry I did what I did. I regret the pain I put you through and I apologize for lying about it. That only made it worse. It was a selfish act and I did not consider the impact on you. I am willing to do what it takes to get your trust back. When I have done that, I would like you to forgive me, but not before then, because I will not have earned it until then."

Yes, this marriage can be saved, but this workbook is not about that. This workbook deals primarily with the healing of the person who had the affair. This is of utmost importance in a marriage. If this person does not heal quickly and thoroughly, they are likely to continue the hurting and going down the path of destruction. Early repair is easiest and most efficient. You want this person to heal. It is in the best interests of all involved.

The deeper goal is that they will realize what led up to it and ensure that it does not happen again.
They will be able to heal their own wound and comfort themselves when they ask, "What else am I capable of doing?"

Major resources

John Gottman   the New Science of Love Principia Amoris Also - The Science of Trust
Janis Spring   After the Affair
Shirley Glass   Not Just Friends
Sue Johnson   Hold Me Tight

"Don, he cheated on me. He lied, and covered it up. We slept together, while he was sleeping with his slut. I can't believe he even gave me this STD! I have been faithful to him and he even had the gall to try to pin the STD on me."

"He won't tell me why he did it. I asked him direct questions. He keeps responding 'I don't know.' How lame is that?"

"He got his mistress pregnant and even tried to hide that at first. Now, we have to deal with another baby. The baby is innocent, but I am having a hard time with this whole situation."

"How many women did he sleep with in this short marriage? I know a few, but I can just tell there are more."

"I cheated on him and he still didn't leave. What will it take for him to leave, Don?"

"I am not the type of woman who does this, but I did this."

Each of these quotes are from a different set of couples. They are trying to repair the marriage or at least were trying until it got so bad that they could not fathom repairing it.

In my experience with couples, those who admit and take responsibility for their behavior tend to go on to a much healthier marriage. They talk about the deeper patterns in their marriage and they work together to bridge the differences. They apologize for quite some time and do a ton of reassuring. That's one way to show remorse and regret and owning the problem.

May you find a solution that works for the highest good of all involved.

Why Did I Do What I Did?

Let me start by saying I appreciate the courage to look at yourself and face your fears.

You may not like some of what you see. Stay the course. Your partner might not appreciate you very much throughout this process. You are not alone. There are many, many people who have violated promises (cheated) and while for a short time in the role of villain, they have struggled. They have gone on to do wonderful things.

This event or process does not define who you are. It is part of what you have done, not who you are. Please remember that. You are multidimensional. You have a context.

Having said that, I do not want to let you off the hook. You had a choice. You always have choices. You chose what you chose. Own that. Take responsibility.

NOW, make the next choice and move on. Too much guilt is not healthy or productive.

My ideal is that you have enough guilt to feel the pain, get the idea that you messed up and then move on with your life so that you do not do it again.

Too much guilt, in my professional experience, actually predicts you will do the bad behavior again.

I have no idea why you did what you did. We may never know. There are many reasons that people give. Let's take some guesses, though. While stating that there is a context, I remind you that you always had the choice to not do it.

My first guess is that you did not feel valued, appreciated and you started to not value the relationship itself. This made it easier to put yourself into dangerous situations. Your partner didn't seem to have your back or listen or even like you a whole bunch of times.

Your partner blew you off and ignored you repeatedly. Or maybe the fighting and name calling was really tough and when it came time to be physically intimate, it just didn't happen.

You thought maybe you could get a better deal from someone else, maybe that person at work who always listened to you. You started comparing your partner to your coworker and your partner came up short, maybe. You started talking about the relationship to this person and they helped your feelings of loneliness. You started being really open with the coworker and eventually threw your partner under the bus. That is how it often goes. The coworker comes back with "I would never have treated you that way." I'm guessing that sounded good to you.

Up to this point, it is often invisible that you are at high risk. Most people don't realize they are in the danger zone until this happens. All they know is that they feel better than they have in quite some time. The friendship with your partner is going south and you may even feel like just roommates and along comes this new friend. All you are doing is talking and getting support.

You can see how dangerous that is, right? At the time it was happening, though, it seemed harmless.

Please go back through this and put a star * next to what applied to you in the early stages of what Gottman calls the Cascade of Distrust. You are not building trust with your partner on this particular path. You are focusing on what is wrong with the relationship, with your partner. This is what we label as an emotional affair. You are getting emotional relationship needs met outside the relationship.

Be brutally honest with yourself.
What would it have taken at this point to be honest with your partner?

Go ahead and answer that question, even if not on paper. It helps!

Looking back on things at this stage, what could you have said to your partner to get off the path to betrayal?

What could you have done differently to get back to the healthy path?

How did you justify staying on this path? What words did you tell yourself to convince yourself that it was not that bad or you deserved it or you were not doing anything wrong?

Can you write the rest of the story leading up to the physical affair with what you have read above?
Go ahead and outline it below at least:

Okay, so at this point, leading up to the affair, have you already changed some habits? Which ones?

Are you wearing new underwear or shirts or perfume/cologne yet?

Are you "covering" or sneaking what you are doing? Some part of your brain knows that sneaking means you should not be doing it.

Have you started with the little secrets at this point in your own story?

Are you at the point in the story where you figure you can't get a fair shake from your partner, so you stop trying to tune in? "It's just not worth it. Don, if I knew how to do this, I would. Please help!"

How about the part where you realize you really do not have their back because you think they don't have yours?

Are you having any self-pity at this point?

Are you able to have a positive outlook on your partner?

Are the two of you having rough fights (verbally)?

At this point right here, the loneliness tends to build to the point that you are vulnerable to having another relationship.

Look how many steps it took to get to this point. Now we are at the crisis point. If you do not turn back now, it is significantly easier to have an affair. You can still turn back.

"I don't understand why I don't want to be intimate and why I withdraw into my cave."

Take your own inventory at this point. Do you recognize yourself in these? Put a * next to the ones you identify.

Is this the pattern you had or was yours different? If different, please describe.

Now we see courtship activity at an all-time low-fun, romance, playing. You pull back from sex with your partner. In the past, you wanted all this with them and you have convinced yourself you do not want it *if it has to be with them*. Some people note they have no loyalty to the relationship itself. *It has lost its value to you.*

The idea of having another relationship is no longer taboo and may even seem like it must happen if you ever want to be happy again. I see this as another crisis point for the couple. Recovering from this step takes significant effort.

Now is when new friendships emerge, usually innocent at first, but dangerous to the relationship. Secrets and sneaking become more common in this phase and this is before there is physical intimacy.

Does this match what happened for you? What was similar and what was different?

The idea is to be really open and honest with yourself. If it did not match, that is fine, let's be aware of patterns so you can avoid those patterns in the future.

Bigger secrets are kept from the partner now. Outright lying and deception are justified. Since you feel like you are not getting legit needs met inside the relationship, it occurs to you that you have *no other option* but to get your needs met outside the relationship.

<u>You now *give yourself permission*</u> to cross boundaries and a deeper betrayal happens.

You start *living* in a world where you have to deceive to keep up appearances

Do you have a better answer when your partner asks, "Why did you do this?"? Could you write the whole narrative now, if asked?

Tell me how the context helps you realize yourself how you got here. Does it help with the guilt you have felt?

NOTE: Some people have misunderstood the above to be *blaming the partner* for the affair. No way. You are responsible for your behavior and they are responsible for their behavior. It is reminding you that nothing happens in a vacuum. There was a context; it did not happen out of the blue. You still had a choice to break off the relationship before having another relationship. You can now hopefully explain it better, it does not justify either person's choice. Again, a thank you to John Gottman for his research on this.

We have the narrative, a deeper understanding. Now we ask for a plan and the work necessary to prevent it, then we are ready and eligible for forgiveness.

Questions to ask yourself:

How do people who have had an affair stop themselves from having a second affair?

Please look at the previous page for that answer. Don't go down the path of betrayal.

When you see yourself heading in that direction, stop and turn around. Talk to your partner. If you cannot get your needs met no matter what, end the relationship and heal.

Then and only then, consider a new relationship.

PLAN: What is your personal plan at this point in the workbook to ensure it does not happen again? (Hint: See where you started the path toward distrust and put an obstacle there.)

1

2

3

4

5

What do I do if I cannot admit to myself what I have done?

If you mean you feel really guilty and ashamed of your behavior, the best I can do is say to *feel it and then let it go*. Allow the feelings to evaporate once they have done their job. When I do things that are wrong, I <u>want</u> my conscience to tell me I should feel guilty.

It keeps me from doing it again. If you are having a hard time letting go of the guilt or if it seems higher than it should be, talk to someone about it.

"I would rather die than deal with this," someone told me. I have a YouTube on forgiveness - Go to YouTube, search "Don Boice Forgiveness." Then get yourself in for counseling.

I get wanting to kill the part of you that did this, but wanting to die is beyond the scope of this workbook. Wanting to kill yourself is a serious sign; please do not ignore it. Get some face to face counseling, please. Try also "Brad Yates YouTube guilt tapping"

PLAN: Be honest with yourself and your level of guilt/forgiveness. What is your plan as of today, to move into a healthier relationship with yourself and guilt?

1

2

3

4

What if it was the perfect storm?

The person had good boundaries, normally. Life kicked them down repeatedly and the person did something uncharacteristic. There was too much pressure and they caved and had an affair.

I like Dan Millman's internet article entitled "The Law of No Judgment." I highly recommend it.

Perfect storms do happen. Rare, but it goes into the chaos theory. The storm is there to shake things up and as you reorganize after the storm, you decide what stays and goes and hopefully you reorganize on a deeper level and come out of it ahead.

What is (or would be) your personal perfect storm?

PLAN: What is your plan if you find yourself besieged or overwhelmed by the perfect storm?

1
2
3
4
5

Q & A

You referenced "Dangerous situation" a few times. What does that mean for you, the reader?

For me, the author, "dangerous situation" is any situation that could lead to an affair if I stayed too long or if it happened at the wrong time.

I do not want an affair, ever. They are wickedly painful and disorienting. I had someone ask me how long I could last if my favorite movie star was attempting to seduce me and I could not get away. Frankly, I hope I never know the answer to that question. Knowing that I am weak is my strength. I would be running away from her. Maybe 5 minutes on a good day?

PLAN: List your top 5 danger zone situations and how you are managing those.
1

2

3

4

5

What is the role of punishment?

After the affair, many people do not feel adequately punished and put themselves through a rough time. Sometimes their own punishment outweighs anyone else's sense of how bad the behavior was.

What do you think is adequate punishment for what you did? Go to your best friend and ask if the punishment matches the crime.

PLAN: How have you attempted to punish yourself?

1

2

3

4

Did they get the job done for you?

What do I do if the other person makes threats of exposure?

If you mean blackmail, you are in trouble. They could expose it at any time and you are vulnerable if it is a secret. When I worked in the addictions field, there was a saying, "You are only as sick as your secrets."

Tell your counselor about the threat. Get it more into the open and it has less power over you. Talk it through and look at it from multiple angles.

"No way, I will take this to my death bed," he told me. That is fine, just know that you are giving it more power than you need to give it. You have to look at you. You have to reconcile it and doing it with a counselor gives you a safe environment for that.

PLAN: Sometimes people do blackmail one another emotionally or for money. If the other person were to blackmail you, what would you do to protect yourself and your family?

1

2

How do I resist temptation?

There are multiple ways to resist temptation. The easiest one is to realize that we are all weak and to stay the heck away from it.

For example, if your temptation relates to having an affair, stay away from danger zones.

Remind yourself how you felt about yourself after this one.

Another idea would be to let someone know you are entering a high risk situation and call them after, kind of like an accountability partner.

Play it all the way through… it is only tempting because it is promising something. If I acted on it, would it really be that good? Who might I hurt? Would it be worth it in the long run if someone found out? Is this who I really am?

Ask for help. Many people turn to prayer when they are tempted.

Clearly there are many options for resisting the many different temptations that exist.

PLAN: What are your top 3 strategies for dealing with temptation?

1

2

3

What if I still miss the other person?

I encourage people to grieve. Of course, you miss the person or at least who you thought they were. Of course, you feel sad and disconnected and it hurts. Feel the pain and let it evaporate when the feeling has conveyed its message or lesson to you.

PLAN: Get a strategy for managing your grief. Do it mindfully versus just letting it happen or winging it.

Make sure it is really over and the other person knows in no uncertain terms that it is over.

You can ritually ask them to leave.

You can listen to Don's CD with three tracks on Letting Go.

Visualize it releasing

Say goodbye in your mind's eye

Apologize to yourself and everyone else involved, recognizing that hanging on to this person will hurt everyone again.

Journal your feelings and thoughts about it.

Tell someone what you are going through.

Make certain you have forgiven yourself at least once during this process.

Consider the following self-statements:

I struggle to forgive myself and I deserve forgiveness.

I feel guilty and afraid, alone and ashamed and in shock- I can release those feelings.

How did I get myself into this and how can I reconcile this with who I really am?

Guilt means I believe I did something wrong. Shame means I am wrong.

This is simply the start of a process that will go faster if I get myself into counseling now.

I make myself ready for forgiveness by owning up to my role in this.

I accept forgiveness. I take it in on the deepest level.

Would I forgive someone else who did this in their relationship?

Pay attention to how you feel as you read each of the above statements.

PART II

Affair Workbook

Now that you have had some time to integrate the information, process some emotion, let's review these because you are not at the same place as when you started this workbook.

Remember, this is a workbook for the people who had the affair, not the person who is cheated on.

Let me distinguish between an emotional affair a physical affair and a sexual affair. When I do something when I get certain emotional needs met outside my marriage/relationship I am having an emotional affair. There are certain needs that have to be met inside of the relationship. When you go outside the relationship to meet those needs you were cheating.

You're cheating if you have an agreement on what needs are met inside it and what needs are met outside. I had one person suggest that going to a counselor is similar to getting your needs met outside of the relationship. "It is like you were an emotional prostitute instead of a sexual prostitute as a counselor."

While there may be some truth in there, the needs that are getting met with the counselor should not be the same needs that can be only exclusively met by the romantic partner.

I have had people say that it was not an affair because there is no sex involved. There were some romance; there is touching but it was not sexual. Be careful with this line of logic because our brains sometimes try to trick us.

Ask yourself these clarifying questions:

*Were you doing the right thing?

Would you have been proud to do this behavior in front of your romantic partner?

If you saw your partner during that same behavior with someone else, would you be okay with it?

Were you sneaking around doing it afraid to get caught?

Denial is *not consciously* lying to ourselves, perhaps but we're not being honest with ourselves.

"I only gave her a back rub. It's the same thing that a massage therapist would do."

I would argue with this person that their intent was not the same intent as a massage therapist. The behavior was identical perhaps but the motivation was qualitatively different.

There's also a slippery slope phenomenon. We may start with behaviors that are perfectly okay and we find ourselves growing attached to the person. We may find that we excuse our behavior, we have a blind spots or were in denial.

We may not realize that we have crossed the line until we have crossed the line. At that point, it becomes very difficult to go back across the line. And we find justifications- I am not the kind of person who does this. And yet I just did that.

With a sexual affair this sort of delusion or denial does not exist. We know that we're not supposed to have sex with someone other than a romantic partner, unless you and your partner have an open relationship. This includes touching sexual parts of the other person sending sexual messages pictures etc. we know when we have crossed this line.

Guilt

Immediately after an affair there tends to be a lot of guilt. With guilt comes punishment and consequences. Karma is simply saying that cause and effect exist. It's not like somebody is punishing us. It's like jumping out of the second-story window and breaking our leg -gravity did not punish us.

When people feel guilty and they have not been caught and punished they tend to punish themselves. They push away the person that they love, push away support; they isolate themselves. They may lose weight. They may gain weight and they do other things to punish themselves. They may withhold or not receive love as well. People who feel guilty also tend to project this guilt on to other people. So if I had an affair, I will see you as very guilty. I will not trust you because I know longer trust myself.

Be compassionate with yourself and realize that we all make mistakes. This is incredibly complicated and there are whole courses taught on forgiveness. You made a mistake- apologize for it, make sure it doesn't happen again, and move on.

Apology

Believe it or not you or yourself an apology. You owe your partner an apology as well, but that is obvious.

You betrayed your-self. On some level you lied to yourself, you denied things, you justified, you went against your code of ethics, and you did not walk the walk.

You lacked integrity in your actions. For these things you owe yourself an apology. (Languages of Love website has the Apology Profile- you can take a quick quiz)

How do you apologize and how would you like to hear an apology?
Do you express regret, remorse, do you ask for forgiveness?
Do you promise that it won't happen again?
Do you do something to make sure that it doesn't happen again?

Which part of this apology appeals to you the most?

"I hurt you. I am so sorry that I hurt you. I never meant to hurt you. It was my fault; I did not have to do that. If I wanted to break up, I should've broken up and then pursued that relationship. I wasn't thinking about you and your feelings and the impact it would have and that was wrong of me. If I could do it over again I would do it differently. Please forgive me when the time is right. I didn't have your back when I was doing that. I was only looking out for my interests, not yours. We both deserve better than that. I am going to do my absolute best to make sure that never happens again. I have a plan of action, a strategy to make sure that that does not happen again."

"Why did you cheat on me?"
This is a question that you will hear over and over again. It really kicks some people in the teeth to hear it. For others, they get discouraged and give up.

The question should have an impact, right? You may not be conscious of why you did what you did, just yet. That is not reassuring because if you do not know why you did it, it is really hard to not do it in the future. It scares your partner that you do not know.

Work on your narrative, your story, the meaning of the affair.
Do that now.

It is the story that defines this part of your life for you and your relationship and likely your family. Be honest and do it.

CONTEXT

Affairs have a lot of different reasons depending on the person, the context.

The most common ones that I have seen are that the relationship is simply not working. One party decides that they don't have to have the back of their partner anymore. The relationship is not valuable. The person did not have their back therefore they don't have to have the back of the person on which they cheat, they reason. It is not quite the demonization that happens when going to war but it's saying that this person's needs are not as important as my own.

It makes it very easy when the other person is ignoring you or neglecting you. Easier when there's no real connection and when there's no friendship or when the relationship has dissolved.

There are also affairs we were one person is a sex addict or is acting out even though the relationship is fine. The best metaphor that I can think of is I ate enough chocolate to satisfy myself after dinner and then when everybody went to bed I finished off the cake. It was binge eating, compulsive behavior. There's nothing wrong with the cake there's nothing wrong with the portion, I just felt compelled to finish it.

Sometimes it is a punishment. The other person had an affair so I'm going to get even with my affair.

Sometimes it's greed or selfishness.

I think we focus too much on the behavior and not the motivation. And sometimes people have very big blind spots. The motivation is actually more important than the behavior if you wanted to not happen again. The best way to have it not happen again is to understand it and put obstacles in place to having the affair. To see the pain it caused to everyone involved.

So, what is your 10 second narrative today of why you had the affair?

Obstacles

What obstacles are you going to put in place so that you not lead to the near likelihood of an affair in the future?

Sample obstacles might be:
Length of eye contact
Length of conversation with people to whom you're attracted
Topic and tone of conversation
Physical proximity and touch
Telling your partner about contact with another person
Telling your partner the truth about how connected you feel with them and repairing that relationship

Please place a star next to the ones you will use. Add your own.

Details

The person who's been cheated on him often wants to know the details. They're trying to understand it and put meaning on it. Trying to get closure.

What research shows us is it some details are not helpful and, as a matter fact, can be harmful.

"I can't get that picture out of my head now that I know what they did and how they did it I wish I did not know."

"I didn't need to know the details I needed to know the motivation and how to fix things if they could be fixed. I did however need to know how far they went."

"I needed to know what I needed to forgive. I didn't need pictures in my brain that are now difficult to erase."

What details have you decided to withhold from your partner? (Give generalities not specifics on this page)

For example, "I have not told him in what positions or what locations we had sex" "I have not told her what the other woman looks like" "I didn't tell her it started before the wedding" "I didn't tell her I was in love" "I didn't say it was on her birthday, on Christmas" Work on your motivation for not telling.

Rebuild Trust

How we build trust is that we have one another's back. That means I'm willing to sacrifice my needs to make sure that your needs get met. (John Gottman has a whole book called the Science of Trust)

When you see that I'm willing to put your needs ahead of my needs you to tend to trust me more deeply.

In what ways have you put your partner's needs ahead of your own- this week?

"When you see me behaving selfishly or self-centered, self-absorbed- it's all about me, you tend not to trust me."

"If I do some soul-searching, I realize that my affair was very self-centered. I need to figure out how to not put myself at the center of the universe. I need to figure out how to prioritize their needs and not just cherish my self-interest."

"I need to remove my ego so that it's not all about me."

In what ways are you moving your needs from center stage?

Do you love your relationship enough to protect it?

The Dog House

Communicate to your partner reassurance on a regular basis.

Expect them to be really upset for a long period of time

You earned your spot in the dog house

How long is too long?

"I know I messed up, but that was like a month ago," he told me. I helped him see that perhaps a month was not as long to her as it was to him. Perhaps the Dog House was still appropriate at that point. A year later, with full apologies, counseling and behavioral change is more than likely overkill.

Jealousy

"My husband is still jealous and I haven't cheated in six months! How long will it take before his jealousy ends?"

How long do you think it will be, before he stops looking at her phone, going through her calendar and messages?

How long before being home late does not trigger a response?

Some of the jealousy may be functional- it means the relationship matters. Other parts of the jealousy are part of what drives people away from one another- "You are not going to control me!" Is it truly jealousy or that you are an insecure person? Insecurity is never attractive and yet, after an affair, insecurity is common.

Talk to your partner about jealousy, each person's. Talk about reassurance and what each of you needs. If you are not sure of your needs, try it this way: What am I complaining about? "I can't stand when you are late from work." Now twist the complaint around into what you would like instead. "I would prefer that you be home when you say you will be. If you cannot, I would like a text or call, to let me know you are okay and to calm me down."

List what you need

1

2

3

4

5

List what they need from you.

1

2

3

4

5

Sexuality and Affairs

Sometimes people do not feel comfortable talking about sex. Great book called Hot Monogamy by Pat Love helps to have the conversation- see the survey on page 21

Or read Art of Sexual Ecstasy by Margot Anand- how to reach deeper, more intimate connection via sex

What messages have you gotten about sex that are unhealthy messages?

I.e. "Women don't like sex. They just do it to please men."

"I am too sexual"

"I like sex way too much"

"I am too aggressive in sex and could not do that with my wife, so I seek out a prostitute."

Add your own:

What is healthy versus unhealthy and who determines that?

++Many people tell me that they are unable to overcome these messages on their own. For example, the woman wants a different kind of sexual experience than the man is prepared to offer. He wants the same thing, but not with her because he was given the message that it is not okay or is slutty, so he must not want it with the person he loves. There is a not so funny joke about once people are married, they are family and you do not have sex with family members. Hmmmm

What messages were you taught about desire and sex drive? Seems to work okay when the woman has a lower sex drive but when the man does, things go south much faster! Would it surprise you that 20% of married couples have sex 10 or fewer times each year?

Please talk about your expectations, your needs and wants. Your opinion, your preferences matter. Talk about it and if you struggle, get help talking about it.

Explore this area fully with your spouse. Talk about the stereotypes and fears, as well. How you talk about it could actually make it more intimate and have it be the best you've ever had. Pretending and faking and avoiding have no place in intimacy. Intimacy means allowing yourself to be known.

For example, in the early stages of relationship there is lots of touch that is sexual and lots of touch that is not sexual. Many women say this fades over time and that every time their man touches them, it feels like a request for sex. If the woman is not in the mood when the request comes in, a common occurrence, she brushes it off. She then may be resentful that all he wants is sex and the only time he touches her, he is asking for sex. "There are times I just want physical closeness and not cuddling and not have to take care of him when he feels badly that I said no to sex."

I work with a lot of guys who misinterpret what to do at that point. They stop asking for sex because it seems to annoy the wife and they stop holding hands and sitting close because they have been told that all they want is sex when they touch. Instead of the couple talking about it, they just stop to avoid the possibility of rejection. Next, they get really resentful and still have the same touch needs, the same affection needs, the needs to talk and be heard. Pretending you do not have needs does not work!

Affair Stories With Healing

Sometimes it is helpful to see the person as a monster and take out all your frustration on them. Sometimes it is helpful to pretend we are innocent and the other person is 100% to blame or that you would never do such a thing. Probably, we are all capable of some bad things. Please read the following and see if you can have compassion for the people in the stories.

1. "I was 98 per cent monogamous"
"I did the math, Don. It turns out I was 98% monogamous. Am I a scumbag and a cheater for what I did? My behavior was cheating. I cheated and yet that does not define who I am. It is one part of who I am. I know that I should not have done it. I know that I don't get kudos for resisting temptation every other time. And yet this is only one part of who I am. It is a very small part. That does not take away from the hurt that I've caused; the damage that it caused. I am simply saying that it is part of who I am not my only role/definition. I screwed up. I take responsibility for what I did. I will do everything in my power to not do it again. There's more good than bad in me. I won't minimize what I did and I also won't exaggerate what I did."

"What I did was wrong. There's also a continuum. We kissed and we touched. I told her deep things about me and she told me deep things about her. I fell in love with her. It lasted less than one month. It could have been much worse. It still should not have happened. I know that and yet a part of me is not sorry that it happened. It is like any painful lesson in life -it opened my eyes and I'm grateful for having had the experience. I'm a better person for having had that experience. What I regret is that it hurt you. I'm sorry that it made you question yourself or second-guess yourself. I'm sorry that I snuck around and that I hid it. I'm sorry that it was deceptive and violated the rules of our relationship."

"Don, what I don't get is -why is my violation of the relationship rules and expectations catastrophic and devastating? When she breaks the rules of the relationship they are just minor things in her eyes. It doesn't seem fair.

She blows me off. She doesn't want to spend time with me. She recklessly spends money we don't have. She doesn't listen and she doesn't empathize. She doesn't carry her own weight in the relationship. She doesn't clean the house, she doesn't pick up after the kids or herself and she doesn't discipline the kids. I feel like I'm living with a child instead of an adult. There are many, many expectations and a romantic relationships. She has not met many of those expectations and many of those rules.

She acts like she doesn't like me. She won't kiss me, she won't touch me, and she won't be affectionate. Forget about sex, that's just not happening and she told me that. When she said that -that was the straw that broke the camel's back. If she doesn't want me and if she's not going to meet those needs, that means that I have to be celibate in this relationship, and I don't get a say in that. That is patently unfair and I refuse to live by those rules.

At that point, I should have broken up and pursued other relationships. My problem is I pursued other relationships before I broke up. I don't know, maybe I was too cowardly. Maybe I thought no one would love me. When I realized someone else saw me as valuable and attractive as a mate and here was my partner blowing me off, it just made sense.

It was not like the relationship was perfect until I screwed it up. The relationship was damaged beyond repair and I pushed it off the cliff. If I went to her at that point, there is no negotiating in good faith. If I went to her at that point, I would not have gotten my needs met. But it would've been clear to me that I need to break up the relationship. That was my fault. That is where I went wrong. "

Put a star next to the words or phrases that resonate with you- above and below.

2. Grass greener
"I compared my new shiny relationship with my old baggage laden relationship. Both of us messed up. It was not all his fault. I got bored. I wanted more out of life and relationships. I complained and was relentless. We got complacent. We took each other for granted and stopped courting. I gained almost 50 lbs., maybe just to keep him away. I stopped having sex with him and he would get angry. I take responsibility for what I did. I was wrong. How long can you reject someone before something happens? I refused to talk to him, to go on a date anymore. The kids were my life, and quite frankly I didn't need him. The kids fulfilled every need that I could possibly have. As they grew older, I needed him more and I was furious that he was not there for me. I deserve better, I told myself. And so I looked for someone who "looked better."

I had forgotten that it was me who rejected him. He did not reject me until I basically threw him out of the relationship. That's where it started. He did want me. He wanted to be in a relationship with me and I threw him out. When I rejected him so thoroughly, of course he went on and begin living his own life. I'm surprised that he did not have an affair after how badly I treated him."

3. All or nothing
"I am a hopeless romantic. I wanted flowers and dates and courting and I forgot that I was also supposed to give. I wanted to be a stay-at-home mom but didn't clean, didn't cook and do the laundry and didn't do the things that other stay at home moms did. I excluded my husband I pushed him out of the family. I pushed him out of the marriage. I take responsibility for that. So I got to stay at home with the kids which is really hard work and yet that is what I wanted. Then I complained that he made me stay home with the kids. That was not true. He was not controlling. He had to work a lot of hours to pay for all the fun that we were having. And yet, I complained about his hours and I also complained about the amount of money that he was bringing in when he did not work a lot of hours. I put him in a bind. No one could please me. And then I fell into a depression. And I could not sleep. I was having trouble eating. And then one night at the bar it happened. I was so used to taking and not giving that when this man showed me attention, I just ate it up. I felt justified. I felt I deserved the attention and it didn't matter that I was married. I thought to myself 'I deserve to be happy and if this makes me happy this is what I'm going to do." And then I began to sneak around quite a bit. I am not proud of what I did and yet I did it and I own it."

4. Remember who you are
"I am not somebody who does that sort of thing. And yet I did it. And I made excuses. And I justified. I told myself it was her fault. I told myself it was the other woman's fault as well.
I deluded myself. Well one time when we were sexual, the condom broke. She had told me that she was on the pill but I wanted to be really safe and my condom broke. You know the rest. She got pregnant. And then I had to tell my wife.

What an awful position for everyone all four of us.

Now, when I go and take care of my baby, it causes suspicion. How do I bring that baby around my family? I really screwed up, and as I'm talking to other people I realize that this happens more than people realize. It's not common, it is just not uncommon."

5. Building trust again
"I want to build trust again. I do have her back. Whatever fog I was in, the fog has lifted. After the affair, I've done all the housework that she has asked. I have let her go through my phone and she has all my passwords to all my devices. I have gone to counseling we have gone to counseling together and we did a couples retreat.

The problem is, well, she still gets really jealous and angry. It has been a couple years now and she still acts as if it was yesterday as if the wound were brand-new. I'm getting worn out by this. I know I deserve some of the suspicion and yet I would like it to go away. I feel incredibly guilty every time she has a reaction like that. And I defend myself with anger I show my anger at her and that makes me look guiltier and more suspicious.

I have read all the articles, all the books -of building trust and relationships. I'm really good at building trust and yet she still doesn't trust me and if she looks at my past she has very little reason to trust me. I was such a good liar."

6. Motivate self to do the work
"The relationship wasn't awesome to start with. As a matter of fact, it was good enough but never great.

I don't want to get our old relationship back. I want to get a new relationship with her, a better relationship. She's a good woman and I think we can do this.

Some days it is hard to hard to motivate myself to do the work necessary. And she doesn't make it any easier. I wish she would stop punishing.

How do I motivate myself on those difficult days? How do I make it okay to keep pushing even when I get no return on my investment?
She has said no sex until she trusts me again. I don't think she understands how guys work. I'm willing to sacrifice for her and yet there's a point where the sacrifice that she is asking is too much.

She is not taking any responsibility for that influence she had on me in this whole affair process. I know that I had a choice. I take responsibility for my part and yet my part is only 75%. I wish she would come clean and say "Okay I know I was unfriendly. I know I didn't often turn to you. I didn't listen to you. I had a role in all this. You are not always wrong." That would make such a difference in me being able to motivate myself. But when I see what the future may hold in the amount of work that I have to do it is daunting."

7. Closure and new meaning
Let go
"I am having a really hard time letting go. I know that what I did was wrong.
There are some things my partner did however there really hard to let go of and that led to the affair. I'm not blaming her I'm just saying she had more influence than she realizes.

She wants to keep blaming me and calling me names and I'm not okay with verbal abuse. I will accept my blame and my responsibility. It would be easier for me to do that if she would accept her role in all this.

She wants me to let go of the other woman and yet she won't let go of the affair. It's been two years now and she still brings it up almost daily.

Come to think of it, I bring it up almost daily and my own brain. I don't say anything but I think about it almost daily. I'm really struggling to let it go.

I want to come up with a new story about it to give it meaning I want a new narrative so that it makes sense to me and I can move on and get closure."

8. Grasping
Wishing it were otherwise
"I Love my husband. I don't want to let him go. But he is really pissed after my affair. He can't seem to forgive me. I wish he would just accept my apology and understand that things really sucked. I know I had a choice and I made a poor decision. I know I hurt him and he's a jealous type and does not forgive easily. And yet I want to stay married. I want to work on this. I keep wishing that I could just be happy and that this would go away. I know that is immature and yet I wish things were different.

I keep hearing that I'm pushing too hard and holding onto tight. I need to detach and to let go to pullback to stop grasping.

When I get desperate like this and feel abandoned and neglected by him, I act poorly. He knows that I act desperate sometimes and this pushes him away even further."

What led up to the affair?

By now, you have a story. It makes more sense, even if it is not complete. It is entirely possible that you will never know the entire story or reason. It is reassuring to your partner when you know what happened and why. It reduces the odds of it happening again.

Often times it is the complete breakdown of the relationship. Other times it is a partial breakdown in a particularly sensitive area, such as sex or money, in-laws, a death or the kids. It is almost always because one person has prioritized their own needs. Two people have competing needs and the needs are so powerful that they cannot fully meet them by themselves. They need someone else and at the same exact time, the partner is needy and has nothing to give. This is a recipe for disaster for those couples who do not have good support networks and cannot ask for help. The partner is not expected to meet all your needs, we all know this in our heads. But when you reach out for help and they do not help, for whatever reason, it is hard to bear.

If either one of you does not feel like a priority, you start pulling away. Sure, at first you complain and demand that the other person pay attention or you pout or punish them or whine and sulk if you can't get their attention. You turn up the volume because it really does matter that they pay attention and connect when you are bidding for their attention.

When either one of you puts your needs first, to the exclusion of the other's needs, bad things happen. Cause and effect- if you act selfishly the effect will be pain. We are not wired to be selfish. That is to say, we are least happy when we act in selfish ways. We are happiest when we get our needs met while considering the needs of others and often sacrifice ourselves for others.

Is an affair about sex?

"Don, I have never had an orgasm during sex," she told me in a counseling session.

Sure, I blushed and became a bit self-conscious.

After that, we talked pretty openly. I listened as she described what it was like and how it pained her and that, quite frankly, it was frustrating to have sex knowing it would not end well. She did not look forward to sex and yet she was very sensual.

Her husband said things like, "You just do not like sex."

That did not help her. She liked sex with herself, could easily orgasm then, but something about the relationship and being vulnerable with others made it impossible to get to that point. I have since learned this is much more common, just no one talks about it.

So when he asks for sex and lovemaking and affection, all she can think is how selfish he is. He benefits from sex while she gets frustrated. Every sexual act becomes another sacrifice she makes for him, in her mind.

You can see how this will end poorly. Additionally, due to the sexual abuse, she does not like certain sex things and behaviors. They trigger her. She is shy and was taught to not talk about her own sexual needs.

So she wants to be a good partner and wants him to get his needs met, as well. She cannot figure out how to accomplish this and since they do not talk about it, it becomes a serious problem.

Until he pulls away sexually, not wanting to keep getting rejected and not wanting to put undue pressure on her. He begins to find other women really attractive and one day at work he overhears a woman talking about how much she loves sex and the porn sites she visits. She is really open to talking about it and he likes how adventurous she is.

Abuse

Yes, you are allowed to be angry with me. You are not allowed, without consequence, with impunity, to call me names, to yell at me, to attempt to embarrass me, to say mean or nasty things, to be cruel or verbally abusive. Those are not you "being angry" with me. Those are you punishing and hurting me and have no place in a healthy relationship. Never okay, never excusable and not justified- no matter what.

Anger is that perfectly acceptable feeling that comes right after fear or hurt.

Anger does not justify the unacceptable abuse; that is a choice, a behavior.

Abuse is the choice to behave in a manner that is mean, cruel, damaging, destructive and harmful to other people. For example: name calling, swearing at, yelling at, embarrassing on purpose, and demeaning them

Feeling angry and telling someone that you feel angry is what people who are healthy do.

Every person has felt angry.

Not every person responds with abuse.

You may have had an affair and the person overreacted when they heard about it. It disorients people and strong reactions are common. Do not abuse your partner and do not put up with abuse.

Yes, they will be angry and that you do need to tolerate. You may find that you are angry at yourself as well.

Please go back and talk with your partner about this, about your narrative, about your why and most importantly, how you are going to make sure this will not happen ever again!

Summary:
Thank you for reading, being open and honest with yourself. This is obviously not the end of the process. There's probably layers to uncover and months, if not years, of healing ahead of you.

Remember that counselors can help you with this. Ask them what they do with someone who has had an affair. See if they are judgmental or healing or condoning and choose accordingly.

You do not have to do this alone!